HUNGER
FOR
REALITY

Also by George Verwer

The Revolution of Love
No Turning Back

HUNGER *for* REALITY

How to escape from spiritual pretence
and double-living

GEORGE VERWER

(formerly published as *Come! Live! Die!*)

Authentic

MILTON KEYNES ● COLORADO SPRINGS ● HYDERABAD

Copyright © 1972 by George Verwer

This edition 1977
Reprinted 1979, 1981, 1983, 1986, 1989, 1990, 1993, 1996, 1998, 2002, 2008, 2013

19 18 17 16 15 14 13   19 18 17 16 15 14 13

Authentic Media Limited,
52 Presley Way, Crownhill, Milton Keynes, MK8 0ES
www.authenticmedia.co.uk

British Library Cataloguing in Publication Data.

A catalogue record for this book is available from the British Library

ISBN 978-1–85078–249–0

Printed in the U.K. by CPI Group (UK) Ltd, Croydon, CR0 4YY

DEDICATED TO

JOHN WATTS and **KEITH BECKWITH**

members of Operation Mobilization who encouraged me to put this message into print and who died in an auto crash in Poland in 1965 while fulfilling the Great Commission committed to them by the Lord Jesus Christ.

CONTENTS

INTRODUCTION

FAREWELL TO SCHIZOPHRENIA

No one could say in these days that we Christians are spiritually starved. Through the care and faithfulness of God's servants, we are generously fed, taught, encouraged, pampered, stimulated, supported, nursed along. A religious world of sermons, discussions, magazine articles, hymns, messages, books, meetings, and conferences surrounds us for our participation and growth. Yet we know very well, if we are honest, that these things have all too little effect on our lives. Why is this so?

If we give the matter a little thought, we will

realize that most of us are living in "two worlds." We have split our convictions, activities, and goals into two categories. In the first we place our religious experiences: what we believe; what we sing about; what we pray about; and what we defend in argument.

The second category contains our world of secular values and actions: our use of leisure time; our actions taken to impress people; our attitude towards associates who are better or worse at their job than we are; and how we get our money and use it.

We keep these two worlds strictly apart, and though we may vaguely feel that something is wrong, we don't suspect we are suffering a major disorder — a sort of spiritual schizophrenia. In church, and occasionally among Christian friends, we talk about dedication, commitment, surrender, revival, a life on fire for God, and other expressions of loyalty and love for God. But the words and their corresponding deeds get little exposure outside church walls.

This evangelical dichotomy has had more serious results than we admit. It has produced men who are hard to get along with, women who rank themselves by the furnishings of their house and the style of their clothes, and whole families that put on smiling faces with their Sunday clothes for a few hours at church.

The late A. W. Tozer commented on this situation in his book *Of God and Men.*

"Evangelicalism as we know it today . . . does produce some real Christians . . . but the spiritual climate into which many modern Christians are born does not make for vigorous spiritual growth. Indeed, the whole evangelical world is to a large extent unfavorable to healthy Christianity. And I am not thinking of modernism either. I mean rather the Bible-believing crowd that bears the name of orthodoxy. . . .

"We are making converts to an effete type of Christianity that bears little resemblance to that of the New Testament. The average so-called Bible Christian in our times is but a wretched parody of true sainthood. Yet we put millions of dollars behind movements to perpetuate this degenerate form of religion, and attack the man who dares challenge the wisdom of it."

Everywhere I go I find young people who are aware of this split of Christian and secular values. Many have become atheists or agnostics because of it, while others have skidded into pits of indifference. Many Christians — leaders included — have admitted to me that their beliefs do not control their everyday lives.

Yet many are hungry for reality and genuineness in the Christian life. I met a student in an evangelical seminary who was first in his class academically, president of the campus mission group, and chaplain of the student body. In talking with me, he admitted that he had very little heart-knowledge of God, but he longed for a satisfying Christian experience.

Can this dichotomy be ended, this schizophrenia cured? Can Christ really revolutionize your life so it is consistent and productive? The answer is yes. I do not offer a formula to achieve this result, but I can offer the real Christ. I have seen him revolutionize people's lives all over the world.

These Christians once lived in spiritual barrenness, then they honestly faced Christ and confessed their besetting sins that clung from the old life. Jesus transformed them, and he can transform you. It is not a life of perfection, but it is a life of reality. It does not mean a life of ease, but it is a life of joy.

If you're tired of split-level living, ask Jesus to make you a whole person.

WE ARE REVOLUTIONARIES!

The Lord Jesus Christ was a revolutionary! Consider, if you will, some of his most basic teachings: "Love your enemies"; "Do good to them which hate you"; "Bless them which persecute you"; "Whosoever will be chief among you, let him be your servant"; "Lay not up for yourselves treasures on earth"; "Except a man forsake all that he hath, he cannot be my disciple."

Do you suppose that all these ideas fell in with the cultural pattern of Christ's day? Of course not! The people of his day were just as

13

enslaved by the material aspect of living as the people of the twentieth century. But the Lord Jesus broke with any cultural pattern which interfered with the life of sacrificial love which he came to give!

In the history of Christianity there have been comparatively few who have lived according to the literal teachings of Christ. The early apostles did, of course. And the results for them were suffering, persecution, imprisonment, exile, and death! Does this seem strange? No! These are the normal results of any life based upon the principles set forth by Christ.

Why is this? The answer is simple: the individual who would live this life is of necessity a revolutionary individual, a cultural nonconformist, a "fanatic," if you please! Literal adherence to the principles laid down by Jesus Christ would, without a doubt, result in worldwide revolution — a revolution motivated by love, a revolution executed by love, and a revolution culminating in love!

And we *are* revolutionaries! We are only a small group of Christian young people in Operation Mobilization, yet we have determined by God's grace to live our lives according to the revolutionary teachings of our Master. Within the sphere of absolute, literal obedience to his commands lies the power that will evangelize the world. Outside this sphere is the nauseating, insipid Christianity of our day.

We have committed ourselves in reckless abandonment to the claims of Christ on our blood-bought lives. We have no rights! Every petty, personal desire must be subordinated to the supreme task of reaching the world for Christ. We are debtors. We must not allow ourselves to be swept into the soul-binding curse of modern-day materialistic thinking and living. Christians have been "willing" long enough to forsake all — the time has come (and is passing) when we must forsake all! Christ must have absolute control of our time and money. We must yield possessions, comforts, food and sleep; we must live on the barest essentials, that his cause might be furthered. The propagation of the faith we hold supreme! Christ is worthy of our all! We must be ready to suffer for him and count it joy, to die for him and count it gain. In the light of the present spiritual warfare, anything less than absolute dedication must be considered insubordination to our Master and mockery of his cause!

This is our commitment, and we will press forward until every person has heard the gospel. We will soon be in many different countries, engaged in combat with all the forces of darkness. We look beyond the thousands to the millions; beyond the cities to the countries. The world is our goal! And our primary targets are the seemingly impenetrable areas of the Communist and Moslem countries which can only receive freedom as they have opportunity to receive the Truth. These countries will be reached for Christ no matter what the cost. The ultimate victory is ours!

We must say to you, fellow Christian, that we are risen with Christ; we seek those things which are above, where Christ sits on the right hand of God. We have set our affections on things above, not on things on the earth, for we are dead and our life is hid with Christ in God. What blessed hope! What *compelling truth* to lead us to total abandonment of self and unto Christ! Without this, there is certain victory for the enemy and disgrace to our Lord Jesus Christ, who gave himself for us that he might be all things to us!

> (This manifesto for world evangelism, with minor changes here, was drawn up by twenty-five students in 1961, the beginning of Operation Mobilization, which the author now coordinates).

2

HUNGRY DISCIPLES

Anyone who claims to be a disciple of Jesus Christ should be experiencing the reality of 1 John 2:6 — "He that saith he abideth in him [Christ] ought himself also to walk even as he walked." Without question, it is God's will for Christian disciples to live as Christ lived. This is not dry theory or a casual observation about Christian living; it is the dynamic standard which produces a vital witness for Christ to lost men and women.

Sometimes the men of the world are wiser in human affairs than the men of God. The agnostic

H. G. Wells said in his *Outline of History*: "Not long after Jesus Christ died, those who claimed to follow him gave up practicing his revolutionary principles." Yes, "revolutionary" was his description, and how right he was! The church has held on to structures and many of the doctrines, but it has lost the core of truth that Jesus taught.

Today you can meet more and more "say-evangelicals" as distinct from "be-evangelicals." As I have visited Bible school after Bible school and Christian institution after Christian institution, I have found many "talkers" of Christianity — but few *walkers!* Not only I, but many Christian young people are acutely aware of this discrepancy. Many have been disillusioned by this contradiction between faith and life.

If we are informed, we realize that many of the young people who grow up in evangelical churches deny the faith before they are twenty-five. We wonder why, and some say, "It must be the latter days" — the days of apostasy and doom. That may be true, but that would not be sufficient explanation of our tragic losses to Satan.

Some Christians say the answer is in "good, sound, Bible teaching." But that is not enough, either. Never in the history of the church have there been so many Bible conferences, radio Bible studies, and Bible study books. Did you

18

know there are more than a thousand books available in the English language on the Pauline epistles? And today we have excellent recorded Bible studies as well. You can hear outstanding Bible teachers in your home by the turn of a radio knob.

We have every opportunity for learning of the life and teachings of Paul, but where are the Pauls of the twentieth century? Where are the men prepared like him and his companions to face cold and shipwreck and robbers for the gospel's sake, and to thank God for the stripes that tore their backs? We have many sincere servants of God and many great preachers. But where are those who can say with Paul that he ceased not to warn men and women night and day with tears? Such men are difficult to find, if not impossible. Why? The reason, I believe, is that we have separated our Bible beliefs from our daily living. Paul never did this.

We want to serve the Lord, and we say, "I am ready to serve the Lord if only I can find my place in his service!" Not finding it, we are frustrated. What is wrong?

God is far more concerned about your finding your place in Christ himself than your place in his service. The essential thing in Christian living is not where you are going or what you are doing, but in whose strength you are living. You may go behind the Iron Curtain or just across the street to serve the Lord, but *in whose strength are you going?* Let us see how the Apostle Paul went about it. In Acts 20:19 we read of his "serving the Lord with all humility of mind, and with many tears, and temptations (trials) which befell me by the lying in wait of the Jews. I kept back nothing that was profitable unto you, but have showed you, and have taught you publicly, and from house to house."

Notice the words: "with all humility of mind." The apostle does not say he is serving the Lord with great preaching, literature distribution, tremendous campaigns behind the Iron Curtain, and great exploits in Turkey and India. He says that he served the Lord with many tears and trials. Discipleship is first of all a matter of the heart. Unless the heart is right, everything else is wrong. Our hearts need to experience a deep hunger and longing for God.

Hunger for God is the genuine mark of a disciple. It confirms to me that I am his child and that he is working in me. What *I do* for God does not prove that I am a disciple. I may try to fulfill the terms of the Sermon on the Mount or of church creeds; I may live ruggedly and sleep on the floor; but these things do not mark me as a disciple. The way I may know I am a disciple is my having an intense, insatiable hunger for the crucified Lord of Glory. If this is your experience — if you yearn for deep fellowship with your Creator, if you desire to know him intimately and to walk with him and to breathe with him — though you may look like a failure and have made innumerable blunders, then you are well on the road to discipleship.

David was an Old Testament individual who knew God and walked with him. Did God say: "David was a man who lived in purity all the days of his life"? No, God said that David was "a man after my own heart."

As we see in the Psalms, David had a hunger for God. "My heart longeth, yea, fainteth for the living God." "As the hart panteth after the water brooks, so panteth my soul after thee, O God." Despite David's failures and backsliding, he was hungry and thirsty for God. In church history right back to the beginning, we find that the mark of a true disciple, a man of God, is a hunger to know God and his righteousness.

The man after God's heart is described in Psalm 34. He can praise God for all his experiences. "I will bless the Lord at all times! His praise shall continually be in my mouth. My soul shall make her boast in the Lord: the humble shall hear thereof, and be glad. Oh, magnify the Lord with me, and let us exalt his name together. I sought the Lord, and he heard me, and delivered me from all my fears" (verses 1-4). And verse 10: "The young lions do lack, and suffer hunger; but they that seek the Lord shall not want any good thing." *They that seek the Lord*: to seek and hunger for him; to praise him continually; these are the marks of a true disciple of Jesus Christ.

Outward marks are often deceptive. The clever Christian, the one who excels in fluent praying or vigorous preaching, or the one who can answer all the theological questions, is not necessarily a disciple. Nor is it necessarily the one who has sold everything, down to the last shirt, in an act of "true discipleship." These things of themselves do not draw us close to God. But God draws near, the Scripture says, "unto them that are of a broken heart, and saveth them that are of a contrite spirit." No discovery of Christian truth has brought more encouragement to me than this one.

Do you remember Jesus' parable of the two men who came to the temple to pray? The first one went to the front and, surveying his audiance, exulted, "O God, how thankful I am that I am not like that other man!" He may have remembered the rich man who turned away from Jesus because he had too many possessions, and then prayed: "God, I thank you that I am not like him, either. No Pharisee would do that!" Perhaps he thought of a young fellow who had never gone on a Pharisee Crusade, inspiring him to declaim: "Thank God I am not like that!" And then he unrolled a beautiful prayer that he learned in the Pharisee Bible College and arranged himself gracefully round the microphone to pray it to his public. But the second fellow, away off in the distance, bent over abjectly and beat his breast in agony, imploring: "God, have mercy on me."

To whom did God draw near? To the theological discourser, tossing out weightless words? Certainly not! As he strode off in his robes of self-righteousness, he knew nothing of God's justification or blessing.

God drew near to the one who came with a broken heart and contrite spirit. He heard the cry: "God, you know I am a failure. You know I am a phony. You know that I am worthless. I am a sinner! Have mercy on me." That man acknowledged his sins, and God justified him. This conflicts with our human understanding, yet it is one reason why I believe the Bible: no man would originate this way of salvation. This shows us the heart of God.

Except for Christianity, every religion offers a combination of service and reward: Do this and you will get that. So the average person would reason that if you are a good disciple of Jesus and live according to the Sermon on the Mount, or if you join evangelistic campaigns and hand out tracts, or perhaps if you shine the shoes of some person to prove how humble you are, then you will be rewarded with great blessing. But blessing comes only by God's way, not man's.

You, by yourself, can never shine anyone's shoes without false motives. You will not even distribute tracts without some personal ambition. Paul asked the Galatians: "Having begun in the Spirit, will you now continue in the flesh?" Many Christians are trying to do that. "I am saved by grace," they might say, "but now I must work my way through the Christian life."

This is a serious mistake. You are saved by God's grace, and by his grace you must serve. The Lord is near — not to the successful but to those who are of a broken heart. He saves — not the energetic but those who have a contrite spirit.

"Delight yourself in the Lord," says the psalmist, "and he will give you the desires of your heart" (Psalm 37:4). The reason we often fail to find the will of God is that we delight in other things. Christians engaged in evangelism are tempted to delight in the adventure of it. Or we delight in the fellowship of the gospel and the enthusiasm we share. I assure you that if you delight in any work for God or in any organization or movement, discouragement will sooner or later catch up with you. Our God is a jealous God, and he will not share his glory with an organization or a personality or movement, however spiritual.

This is so clear in John 5:44, when Jesus says to disbelieving Jews: "How can you believe, which receive honor one of another, and seek not the honor that comes from God alone?" How can you believe God for great things — for laborers, for finances, for conversions, for victories in the lives of Christians — when you seek honor from other humans?

While we seek honor for ourselves, or try to advance the program or reputation of a movement or a preacher, we are building on the fragile merit of men. As the mark of a true disciple is his hunger for God, his goal is God's approval. When the work is done, he wants to hear God say, "Well done, thou good and faithful servant." Day after day he lives for God and his glory, seeking it as the deer craves the water of the brook.

Despite the weaknesses of Christ's people, there are many today who are hungry for God. This hunger must be cultivated both by feeding and by developing its capacity. God wants all of our being, not just our labor for the Lord, or our problem-solving, or our serving behind the scenes. We can get so caught up in activities, even Christian ones, that we lose conscious contact with God himself. He waits, close but silent, ready to remind us: "My child, you are too busy to receive any strength from me."

His counsel remains: "Be still, and know that I am God" (Psalm 46:10). The only way to find the necessary power and resources for each day is to quietly wait on God. Plan for time to be alone with him; learn to delight in him; cultivate a hunger for his infinite being. Without this, your work will be superficial; with it, your deepest desires will be filled and your discipleship will glorify him.

Our situation today is described well in these words by A. W. Tozer:

"In this hour of all-but-universal darkness, one cheering gleam appears — within the fold of conservative Christianity there are to be found increasing numbers of persons whose religious lives are marked by a growing hunger after God himself. They are eager for spiritual realities, and will not be put off with words, nor will they be content with correct interpretations of the truth. They are athirst for God, and will not be satisfied until they have drunk deep at the Fountain of Living Water."

Many things have blinded our eyes; a multitude of theological distinctions and religious traditions have made a dichotomy between the doctrines of God and an intimate relationship with him. But there is hope wherever Christians are hungering for God. They are joined in a crusade to know God. This is the only cause that ultimately counts, the only link that will not be bent and broken by the ignorance and selfishness of men. Our real link is not with any organization, but with the living God. As we humble ourselves at the cross, we shall learn the reality of Jesus' power that conquered sin and death. We will receive the promise: "Blessed are they who hunger and thirst after righteousness, for they shall be filled" (Matthew 5:6).

3

THE PRAYER OF FREEDOM

"Litany" is a word that describes a formal prayer read by church people the same way each time. A great deal of litany was abandoned by the Protestant churches after the Reformation, and almost everything of Roman Catholic origin was rejected by the new churches. This resulted in some spiritual losses that we couldn't really afford, because some of the devout Roman Catholics can teach us vital truths. The power of the gospel and the presence of the Lord Jesus Christ infiltrate even somnolent churches, and some people come to know him and love him just as Martin Luther did within the Roman

Church. If we Protestants possessed some of the spiritual depth evidenced by men such as Francis of Assisi, I believe we would accomplish far more for the Lord.

I do not know the name of the Roman Catholic who wrote the following litany, but it speaks of a life that all disciples of Christ need to experience.

> "O Jesus, meek and humble of heart, hear me. Deliver me, Jesus,
> from the desire of being loved,
> from the desire of being extolled,
> from the desire of being honored,
> from the desire of being praised,
> from the desire of being preferred to others,
> from the desire of being consulted,
> from the desire of being approved,
> from the fear of being humiliated,
> from the fear of being despised,
> from the fear of suffering rebuke,
> from the fear of being forgotten,
> from the fear of being wronged,
> from the fear of being suspected.
>
> And, Jesus, grant me the grace to desire
> that others might be loved more than I,
> that others may be esteemed more than I,
> that in the opinion of the world others may increase and I may decrease,
> that others may be chosen, and I set aside,
> that others may be praised and I unnoticed,
> that others may be preferred to me in everything,
> that others may become holier than I, provided that I become as holy as I should."

If we sincerely prayed like this every day, I am sure the Holy Spirit would marvelously change our lives. I believe the qualities spoken of in this prayer can become ours today. This should be our goal, not the accomplishment of any particular task for God.

There are many cheap substitutes and secondary roads for genuine holiness. We can tramp down one false route after another clutching the counterfeit of New Testament discipleship instead of possessing the real thing.

When I was a student, I was hungry to know what Christian holiness was, and I searched the Scriptures to find out the heart of the New Testament message. I came to the profound conviction that the Holy Spirit wants to produce Christlike individuals — not religious robots, not doctrinal champions, not evangelistic whirlwinds, but men who are like Jesus Christ. That is basically what this prayer is about.

These attributes are characteristics of Jesus. He was the one who was not esteemed, who was unloved, who was unextolled. He would not accept honor nor any of the things that ambitious men crave. He was the one who finally was completely despised and consequently executed. This prayer was written by a person who knew God intimately.

The work that God wants to do supremely in our hearts is to produce Christlikeness. It is a work that will take all our lives — there are no shortcuts to this kind of spiritual growth. There is no organization, no activity that can substitute for it. We need a constant hunger and thirst for the nature of Christ to be reproduced in us. We need, too, an awareness of the unending spiritual warfare surrounding us.

Men at war have to be ready to die any day. They may not know Christ, but they are ready to lose their lives as they go out to fight, or they are poor soldiers. We need something of the same spirit in spiritual warfare. We who have Christ's eternal life need to throw away our own lives. This readiness can come as we pray and live in the direction of this prayer.

It begins, "Deliver me, Jesus, from the desire of being esteemed." We all have an innate desire to be esteemed. However undistinguished we are, we like to be recognized. When we meet a new group of Christians and someone says, "Good to have you with us, brother! Would you like to share what God is doing in your life?" we feel gratified. But if we are ignored or slighted, we feel hurt. Whether we are extroverted or introverted, we selfishly desire attention, and so we all need to pray: "Lord, deliver me from the desire of being esteemed." In Philippians Paul warns against the product of inordinate self-esteem: "Let nothing be done through strife or vainglory, but in lowliness of mind let each esteem the other better than himself" (2:3). This requires the love-power of Jesus Christ.

The second petition of the prayer asks: "Deliver me, Jesus, from the desire of being loved." To be loved is our basic psychological need. Children cannot develop normally without love, and adults cannot function happily without the security of love. God met these needs supremely by giving his Son in love for us. "Hereby perceive we the love of God, because he laid down his life for us" (1 John 3:16). The greatest way God could demonstrate his love was to give his beloved, perfect Son to redeem us from sin. And his desire for us is that we should minister that same love to one another, for the same Scripture continues: "We ought to lay down our lives for the brethren."

I believe that some Christians strive anxiously for manifestations of God's love because we do not experience the love of fellow Christians which Christ commanded to be given. When there is little love flowing between us, we may feel impelled to seek special favors and blessings from God as confirmation that we are loved.

God's plan, according to the Scriptures, is for Christians to love one another, even as Christ loved the Church and gave himself for it. The revolution of love is caught and passed on horizontally as well as vertically.

Most men who are on fire for God caught the

spark from another man on fire. Great men of God grew to be like Christ because they had been with a man of God as well as with God himself in communion. God meets us in prayer and in his Word, but he also meets us through the person and example of another brother.

I owe more than I can tell to the love and encouragement of other Christians. One of them is Billy Graham, though I do not know him personally. I have read his life story and followed his progress, and once I shook his hand in a crowd, and I felt his love even there.

I had gone to his office in London on business, and many people were there ahead of me. The whole office force was caught up in the pace of an evangelistic crusade, and nobody had spoken to my friend and me except the receptionist. Then Graham came in and immediately started shaking hands with everybody. He came straight to us and greeted us, and said something very kind. Here is a famous man who is fifty times busier than most people, but he had time to shake hands with the nobodies in his outer office. This was especially heartening to me, because I had found Christ as my Savior through Graham's preaching.

People will come to know Jesus if we go where they are and love them in this way, but the revolution of love cannot spread if we are intent on gaining love from others. We all need love, but the Christian disciple concentrates on giving love because he has received abundant love from God. A severe test comes when we feel unloved and rejected, as Jesus was. But at that crisis we may prove how wonderful the Lord's love is by giving ourselves for others.

The next snare we must be delivered from is "the desire of being extolled." I define "extol" as flattering or praising. How much we enjoy this! It is almost like feasting at a banquet. Jesus, we are told in Philippians, was just the opposite. He was "everything" in heaven, and he became as a criminal on earth. The Bible says: "Except a grain of wheat fall into the ground and die, it abideth alone." In order to be fruitful, the disciple must die to himself. Do not seek to be lifted up; be submerged.

This may be practiced every time we are overlooked or not given credit for our deeds. It is hard on the ego — which is just what the ego needs. This prayer helps to cut us off from the cancerous craving to be somebody, to gain a status superior to others. It checks the treacherous invasion of Satan among Christian workers.

Very close to this is the next plea: "Deliver me from the desire of being honored." God said: "How can you believe which receive honor one of another, and seek not the honor that cometh from God only?" (John 5:44) Jesus' testimony was: "I receive not honor from men." Often when a Christian has accomplished something for God, he is tempted to exploit it for heightened personal honor. This temptation is from Satan. Some honors and recognitions are very subtly harmful. They come from well-intentioned people or Christian organizations, and the commendations become food for self-exaltation. Sometimes we can receive more honor from fellow Christians than from the world system, and the "sanctified" source makes the praise all the more insidious.

There is even a danger of our seeking spiritual experiences for self-aggrandizement. We are tempted to testify of deliverance from sin, or answered prayer, or some other experience of God's grace in a way that brings vast satisfaction to ourselves rather than honor to God. His grace is to be prized, but it is not to be flaunted as a sign of our merit.

I sometimes get letters from young people seeking training, who write recommending themselves. They tell me how great they are, and how many qualifications they have. Can you imagine getting a letter like that from the Apostle John? There *was* of course a time when, like the others, John sought credit and even precedence for having followed Jesus, but that was before the cross brought about a revolution in all their lives. It is not wrong to be encouraged. What is wrong is the seeking of praise and commendation from others. Do we praise God as much when we are alone as when we're with others? Do we continue our work alone with as much enthusiasm as we did when we were being observed? I dislike working alone and believe in working two by two. But sometimes we are alone, and then we are tested as to whether we are concerned for our honor or for God's.

The next prayer is very close in meaning: "Deliver me from the desire of being praised." This is related to everyday associations and deeds. If we are hungry for praise, we eagerly accept crumbs of approval from anyone, whether they are sincere and honest or not. Such praise turns rotten on the tongue of fickle and unprincipled men.

We also pray: "Deliver me from the desire of being preferred to others." How do we feel when we are qualified and someone else is chosen? Do we rejoice when a fellow Christian receives honor? This blessing to another may cut us deeply. A. W. Tozer said, "The cross will cut into our lives where it hurts the worst, sparing neither us nor our carefully cultivated reputations." Worldly men put great stock in their ranking, but John the Baptist easily declared: "He that cometh after me is preferred before me."

"Deliver me, too, from the desire of being consulted." Our experience and knowledge are hindrances when we expect others to defer to us and acknowledge our wisdom. Being overlooked is especially trying when our advice seems to be so obviously right. But this is another form of self-serving, as we can trust God to employ our advice if it is needed for his glory.

Most of us need deliverance also from "the desire of being approved" — of being assured by others that we were right, after all. Disciples must continue to be learners in God's school of life. When people ask me what degree I am studying for, I reply "The A.U.G. — Approved Unto God." It will not be awarded in this life, but it is the only one that matters eternally.

A common burden we carry is "the fear of being humiliated." We want to "look good" to others, even desiring to make favorable impressions "for God." But God does not have this problem — in his perfection and power, he is never humbled. And his Son did not shrink from the humiliations of men when he was on earth.

God often takes us the same way his Son went. The humiliations dramatize the contrast between God's ways and man's, and point the way to safety. Records show that swimmers who have practiced life-saving are vulnerable to drowning because they are overconfident in the water. God would save us from overconfidence in self, and so he humbles us. He undermines and weakens our naturally strong points for our good and our

37

growth in him. Let us not fear the humiliation that can bring this valuable benefit.

Deliver us, too, Lord, from "the fear of being despised." Oh, how we need this fearlessness for witnessing. So many people scorn the Christian who witnesses for Christ. The distributor of tracts may be despised, but we who know their value should give them out as though they were bank notes. Some people resent the "invasion of their privacy" concerning spiritual matters, but the Christian witness is investing in eternity. May God's love fully cast out this fear.

The "fear of suffering rebuke" clutches at most Christians, yet we need correction to avoid lagging in our discipleship. Christians must learn to speak to one another both in love and rebuke. Though we learn primarily from the Spirit of God, he may use a brother or sister to teach us. Earnest disciples can expect God to speak through his Word, through prayer, and through the exhortations of a brother.

God has given me, I believe, increasing grace to take rebukes, but it has taken years. I reacted like a rattlesnake to the first rebukes I got as a Christian. There's a great difference between a rattlesnake and a worm. The Bible compares Jesus to a worm in the treatment he received (Psalm 22:6). If you strike a worm, it wriggles or dies, but if you strike a rattlesnake, you are struck in return. How significant it is that Satan is described as a serpent!

Our twenty-five reasons why the other fellow is wrong and we are right are always near the tip of our tongue. But our readiness or reluctance to defend ourselves is a measure of our spirituality. Let us implore God to make us unafraid to receive rebukes.

Then there is the almost universal "fear of being forgotten." In India, where living conditions are so poor, some people hoard money to make sure a beautiful memorial over their grave will remind the living of their name. Some Christian churches also are filled with memorials that perpetuate the names and prestige of the dead.

Most of us fear being forgotten by friends. If we don't struggle to prove our worthiness or helpfulness, our past contributions may be forgotten — and us too.

But life is not lived in the past. Service, satisfaction, and sharing are experienced in the present. Forgetting the things that are past — though we can never forget the people — we press on for today's goal. Let us fear being remembered only for the past. God remembers every good thing we do, and that's sufficient.

"Deliver me, Jesus, from the fear of being ridiculed." Wise is the person who can laugh at himself! Sometimes there is such good cause! Sometimes the ridicule is malicious and is intended to hurt. It may be difficult to realize at such times that the ridicule is a boomerang, injuring the source. The Bible says: "The Lord looks on the heart," and if my heart is right I may be filled with peace. As we bare our hearts to him, he is quick to reassure when man is quick to ridicule.

"The fear of being wronged" may keep us from trusting people. This fear can be crippling, preventing us from taking a step of faith immediately before us.

The closely related "fear of being suspected" immobilizes some Christians. But we are always going to be misunderstood by someone, no matter what we do. Praying often in meetings will cause some to think you are trying to display your spirituality. We cannot afford to be bound by fear of what others may think. "Rejoice," said Jesus, "when men shall say all manner of evil against you falsely for my sake." We can come to that place of liberty where, because we love the Lord Jesus and act in faith, we are not anxious about what other people think or suspect.

The second section of this prayer deals with worthy desires. "Jesus, grant me the grace to desire that others be loved more than I." This reminds us of the need people have for love which I can help to supply. Wherever I go I meet people who need love and attention — to be visited, listened to, written to, prayed with. How can this enormous need be met? Only by God's grace working in me that others may be esteemed more than I.

"Grant me the desire that in the opinion of the world others may increase, and I may decrease." The testimony of John the Baptist is unequivocal: "I must decrease." The following phrases of the prayer: "That others may be chosen, and I set aside; that others may be preferred to me in everything; that others may be praised and I unnoticed" are summed up in this principle that Jesus Christ must increase, but I must decrease. I must hide behind the cross, that my Lord may be seen and worshiped. I must recognize myself as nobody, so Jesus will be my All.

The final clause is revolutionary: "That others may become holier than I, provided that I become as holy as I should." There is always a danger that Christians may have such a hunger for spiritual reality that we tread on other people in our search for it. The Christian life is not a competition with others; we have a common goal and we grow together in the strength and grace of the body of believers. We must drink together at the Fountain of Living Water.

Can we honestly pray this amazing prayer? I am reminded of some words of A. W. Tozer that I have written in the front of my Bible:

"The Church at this moment needs men who feel themselves expendable in the warfare of the soul. Such men will be free from the compulsions that control weaker men, the lust of the eyes, the lust of the flesh, and the pride of life. They will not be forced to do things by the squeeze of circumstances. Their only compulsion will come from within and from above. This kind of freedom is necessary if we are going to have prophets in our pulpits again instead of mascots. These free men will serve God and men from motives too high to be understood by the rank and file who today shuffle in and out of the sanctuary. They will make no decision out of fear, they will take no course out of a desire to please, accept no service for financial consideration. They will perform no religious act out of mere custom. Nor will they allow themselves to be influenced by the love of publicity, or by the desire for reputation."

The link between this passage and the prayer is clearly etched. It is as though these two spokesmen, the earlier Catholic and the modern evangelical, learned in the same school. And they have, for they both studied at the feet of Jesus.

4

THE LAND OF REST

If the Promised Land was a country to conquer under the leadership of Joshua, it was also a place of rest and victory for the Israelites. A "Promised Land" also awaits the Christian who is willing to move from the wilderness wanderings of self-effort and frustration.

"Let us therefore fear, lest, a promise being left us of entering into his rest, any of you should seem to come short of it. For unto us was the gospel preached, as well as unto them: but the word preached did not profit them, not being mixed with faith in them that heard it. For we which have believed do enter into rest, as he said, As I have sworn in my wrath, if they shall enter into my rest: although the works were finished from the foundation of the world. For he spake in a certain place of the seventh day in this wise,

And God did rest the seventh day from all his works.

"And in this place again, If they shall enter into my rest. Seeing therefore it remaineth that some must enter therein, and they to whom it was first preached entered not in because of unbelief: Again, he limiteth a certain day, saying in David, Today, after so long a time; as it is said, Today if ye will hear his voice, harden not your hearts. For if Jesus had given them rest, then would he not afterward have spoken of another day. There remaineth therefore a rest to the people of God. For he that is entered into his rest, he also hath ceased from his own works, as God did from his. Let us labor therefore to enter into that rest, lest any man fall after the same example of unbelief" (Hebrews 4:1-11).

So many Christians are carrying burdens. Though we try to drop them or run away from them, they cling like mud on our feet and fear on our mind. These burdens are carryovers from our pre-Christian days, and God intends Christians to be rid of them.

The account of Israel's coming out of Egypt and entering the Promised Land, Canaan, is a graphic picture of the full redemption we have in Jesus Christ. It vividly describes God's intervention into human affairs as well as the variety and complexity of problems encountered by God's people. Paul reminds us that "these things were written for our example."

Moses, the man who received from God the Ten Commandments, inscribed on stone, did not understand God's ways in his earlier years. He did forsake prestige and privilege in the Egyptian hierarchy to identify himself with God's people, but he recklessly asserted himself on behalf of the Israelites instead of acting by God's direction. The result was a forty-year exile in the Sinai wilderness. There, from a burning bush, God called and commissioned Moses to return to Egypt and deliver Israel.

Moses was afraid, so keenly was he aware of his past failure. When God told him to go, he said, "They won't listen to me." He pleaded, "I can't speak. . . ." Moses was like so many ambassadors of God who have begun with: "I'll never be a witness for Christ; I can hardly speak. I'll never be a missionary; I don't like spiders and snakes; I can't sleep on the floor. I'll never do this because I am afraid of that." Yet God did such stupendous things through Moses.

Israel's exit from slavery in Egypt is a picture of the Christian's deliverance from sin's bondage. God's judgment fell on the unrepentant Egyptians but not upon the people who were marked by the blood of the Passover lamb. After the angel of death struck Egyptian homes, Pharaoh capitulated and ordered: "Let them go," and the nation of slaves started for the Promised Land.

They had not gone far before Pharaoh changed his mind and started after them. If Moses thought his troubles were over after getting out of Egypt, his education was just beginning.

Leading one of the largest mobilization operations in history, Moses was doing quite well shepherding a million people and innumerable animals toward the open spaces and safety. Then billowing dust from the fast-moving war chariots of Egypt signalled the pursuit of a vengeful army, and fear swept through the refugees. "Moses," they cried, "you've brought us out here to be killed. Why didn't you let us stay back there? Things in Egypt weren't that bad!"

Hedged in by grumbling people, advancing Egyptian soldiers bent on slaughtering or recapturing them, and rolling waves that blocked their flight, Moses appeared in a desperate strait. But the appearance was deceiving.

Moses cried to God for help, and then obeyed God's command to wait for deliverance. Another miracle took place as the waters of the Red Sea parted and the wind made a dry path for the Israelites to walk over. They hurried across, hardly able to believe their eyes, and the chariots of Pharaoh raced to overtake them. All at once the waters swept back, and chariots, Egyptians, and Pharaoh were gone!

Satan is not finished when Christ first delivers us from his clutches. The night I was converted, I stepped out of Madison Square Garden in New York where I had accepted Christ, and bumped into solid opposition. It was in the form of a belligerent youth anxious to demonstrate his masculinity. I objected to a crude remark made about girls, and this street pugilist deposited me on the concrete with one blow. That was my introduction to the Christian life — I learned early that it's a warfare!

The problems Moses faced in the wilderness were problems every Christian leader has. The people complained about the arrangements, questioned Moses' motives, and wistfully recalled the few pleasures they'd left behind. Somewhat like the twentieth-century Church, they whined, "Of course, we want to be free, but can't we take a little of Egypt with us? We don't want to live back there, but some Egyptian styles can't hurt!"

But God had promised them a place of rest, a land overflowing with milk and honey. He never intends his people to subsist indefinitely on manna rations. The wilderness crossing to Canaan was short, and they could have entered directly. But the advance scouts saw only hazards and enemies in the Promised Land. "There are giants over there," they stammered. "We are like insects in their eyes. We can never possess such a land." And they were immobilized by distrust of God.

Today we hear and see the same disbelief. "It cannot be done!" "There are giants in the land — Buddhism, Islam, Communism." "We must forget the countries closed to the gospel." Like Israel, the Church often does not see that the place of challenge is also the place of rest.

There were two "fools for Christ" in Israel: Caleb and Joshua. They were prepared to believe God and act, and they later entered the Promised Land. The great majority were doomed to wander, struggle, and die in the wilderness. How many men of faith and vision in our generation have pointed to the place of spiritual rest and gone unheeded? Still the Promised Land waits.

We cannot live a life of victory in the "wilderness" of unbelief and disobedience. If we go to serve the Lord in Asia or Europe or America — or wherever — and we go in doubt, burdened with problems and wrestling opposition in our own strength, we shall experience steady failure and discouragement.

Hebrews 4:10 declares that "he that is entered into his rest, he has ceased from his own works as God did from his." Any work for God that depends on our own efforts, our own zeal, our own ability, and resources, will fail. The place of victory and rest is the place of *God's* works, not ours. We are active and completely involved, but the victory does not depend on us and the cause for anxiety is gone.

We can enter into God's rest now because Christ has entered it for us. When we contemplate what Christ did for us on the cross, we realize that God has genuinely identified us with Christ. Through our faith in the One who died for us, we have been "crucified with Christ" — identified with him in his death. If you are a Christian, you have been crucified with Christ! It is not something that can occur in the future if we trust enough, or pray effectively, or memorize another seventy-eight Scripture verses. No, we are to see ourselves dying to sin with Christ on his cross, and as the truth dawns we can find ourselves entering into his spiritual rest just as the people of Israel found the Jordan parted and their inheritance open to them as they crossed over. This entrance takes place when we recognize that Christ is our *All* — our strength, our guidance, our hope, our victory — and although the battle is not over, the anxiety and fear are.

Some people know the exact day on which they were born again. For me it happened on March 5, 1955. Others have just as real an experience, but cannot tell the date of it. They do know it happened. It is the same when we enter this experience of victory — we may not be able to explain it or tell when it happened, but we know that we are in a new relationship to God.

No man can offer truly effective service to the Lord unless he has entered this life of restful trust in God, this victory of the risen Christ. Because then, just as we are truly identified with Christ in his vanquishing of sin and death, so we are identified with him in his risen life. We cease our struggle in self-centered accomplishments and live by the power of Jesus' resurrection. That is real victory.

This is the only way to success in Christian living. It is the way of faith, the same kind of faith that brought us salvation. "The just shall live *by faith*" (Romans 1:17). "As you have therefore received Christ Jesus the Lord, so walk in him" (Colossians 2:6). Then we shall say with Paul, "I live, yet not I, but Christ liveth in me" (Galatians 2:20). When we have entered God's place of rest, we cease from our selfish strivings and the worries that accompany them.

There are times when I have a hundred letters on my desk, many of them about problems. Where should evangelism teams go? Where is the money to support them? How shall we find the vehicles to move teams and literature to their destination? I have learned from 1 Peter 5:7 what to do with them: "Casting all your care upon him, for he careth for you." Sometimes I can say, "Lord, those letters, those telegrams, are all yours. I'm going to bed."

Sleep is a wonderful blessing, and we must not let worry rob us of it. I do not believe in worry because I believe in God's place of rest. I believe that Jesus Christ was crucified for all the worries of the world, and if the Lord Jesus did that, then why should I be anxious about them? This applies to every area of life, every frustration, every inferiority feeling, everything that bothers me. All these things cannot defeat me unless I leave the place of rest — my security in Christ.

As Christians we know that we walk daily in a wilderness world, but the attractions of the wilderness need not walk in us. Whenever they intrude through our eyes or ears or mind, the citizen in the Promised Land must pray: "Lord, I used to enjoy that diversion in slavery, but I have died to that in Christ; hold me in your rest and resurrection life." It is ours for the asking and the trusting.

The Promised Land of rest on this earth is not for sleeping; it is for fighting — but it is the place where you hear God say: "I shall fight for you." Opposition, danger, temptations, and hardships surround you, but your spirit rests in the fortress of God's love and power. Will you choose this sanctuary instead of trying to straddle the Jordan and keep one foot in the world? It's the most important thing you can do in response to this book.

5

FRONT-LINE PERILS

Have you decided to walk the road of discipleship? Are you determined to follow Christ wherever he leads? Then be prepared for obstructions, washouts, and falling rocks! For it is absolutely certain that you have a rough road ahead of you.

One of the ways God helps the disciple is to give a glimpse in Scripture of the perils encountered on the way to a victorious Christian life.

"Moreover, brethren, I would not that ye should be ignorant, how that all our fathers were under the cloud, and all passed through the sea;

and were all baptized unto Moses in the cloud and in the sea; and did all eat the same spiritual meat; and did all drink the same spiritual drink: for they drank of that spiritual Rock that followed them: and that Rock was Christ.

"But with many of them God was not well pleased: for they were overthrown in the wilderness. Now these things were our examples, to the intent we should not lust after evil things, as they also lusted. Neither be ye idolaters, as were some of them; as it is written, The people sat down to eat and drink, and rose up to play. Neither let us commit fornication, as some of them committed, and fell in one day three and twenty thousand. Neither let us tempt Christ, as some of them also tempted, and were destroyed of serpents. Neither murmur ye, as some of them also murmured, and were destroyed of the destroyer.

"Now all these things happened unto them for ensamples: and they are written for our admonition, upon whom the ends of the world are come. Wherefore let him that thinketh he standeth take heed lest he fall. There hath no temptation taken you but such as is common to man: but God is faithful, who will not suffer you to be tempted above that ye are able; but will with the temptation also make a way to escape, that ye may be able to bear it" (1 Corinthians 10:1-13).

Notice particularly that Paul says these experiences are examples "for our admonition." He is warning about the many hazards that beset Christians. Although these Israelites shared in God's revelation of power to Moses in the pillar-cloud and the retreating sea, and though they received the same spiritual sustenance, they failed to pass the stern tests that Moses overcame. In a similar way, the Christian leaves Egypt — the world — and crosses the Red Sea — which speaks, I believe, of salvation. He begins to sing of his liberation, just as the Israelites did when they saw the Red Sea rolled back and the enemy wiped out behind them. But he fails to realize that mighty enemies are still ahead.

Ancient Simeon Stylites lived on top of a flag pole for thirty years, yet he did not escape trials. You may isolate yourself anywhere and still face conflicts. Why? Because the enemy roves within you. The people of Israel fled from the giants of Canaan, but suffered defeat after defeat in the deserted wilderness. Only Joshua and Caleb survived of the pioneer travelers, because they trusted in God.

These two men illustrate the reality of heart commitment to God. They could easily have differed with each other, but their hearts were right with God. Caleb, for example, said, "Let us go up at once, and occupy it; for we are well able to overcome it." Some observers might have accused him of self-confidence, but God knew his faithful intention. Joshua focused his words on God: "If the Lord delights in us, he will bring us into this land and give it to us."

What thrills me is that both men walked with God, both entered the Promised Land, and both were richly blessed. They did not judge the other's motives by a variation in terminology. And neither should we. A young Christian with wrong vocabulary and ill-expressed doctrine may actually be trusting in the work of Christ more than Mr. Deeper-Life who has it all turned out to the last syllable. Caleb's and Joshua's key to entry into Canaan was the same: their sincere, persevering response to God's promise.

I believe the land of Canaan speaks of the Christian's victorious life. The salvation of God has taken us across "Jordan," but most Christians languish on the border of the Promised Land. We stubbornly disbelieve the mountain ascent will bring us to our inheritance, and we hide among the rocks in the valley.

We must go on, though we are not entering a picnic ground or holiday camp when we cross Jordan. Battles, struggles, trials, and defeats are ahead in the Promised Land, but so are victory and joy and power. After truly entering this land, you will know more of God's fullness and power, thrilling answers to prayer, and intimacy of true discipleship. Yet you will be amazed that the battle can be so fierce. At times there may be no more than bare necessities supplied. Here we realize we are in a fight to the finish with sin, self, and Satan.

The realization that we are involved in a constant spiritual warfare can be a great source of strength and comfort. When some difficult situation arises or fiery darts from Satan pierce us, we realize that this is part of God's wonderful plan for us. My wife and I can testify that it is doing wonders for us in our married life. Friends often give advice: "You should do this . . ."; "All parents do that . . ."; but we are able to go on our knees and say, "That's right, Lord, in times of peace, but this is war!"

We are helped when we reflect on this century's two world wars. Think of the demands made upon young men; think of the anxieties suffered by wives and children. And we have been given the privilege of fighting in the battlefield alongside the Lord of glory, the Captain of our salvation. What sacrifice can be too great for him? Compared with what Christ did on the cross for us, our service for God is nothing.

Someone has said, "The devil doesn't waste his fiery darts on nominal Christians." The history of war confirms that armies make opposing leaders their targets. Satan uses the same tactics. He does not waste time on those who are not counting for God; he aims for the active disciple.

When the devil sees someone steadfastly following Christ, he goes into a strategy meeting with the demons of hell and together they plan a full-scale attack. If we understand something of the enemy's movements and are armed against them, we shall not be caught unawares.

Two tactics we are told to use against the devil are to resist and to run. I have always been a better "runner" than "resister," but I want to learn more about resisting in God's strength. The Word of God tells us to "flee" Satan's temptations (2 Timothy 2:22). It says to resist him, not in our own power, but in the power of the cross of Christ (James 4:7). The atoning blood of Jesus Christ removes the guilt of our sin, and the cross severs Satan's control over us. The crucified life of a disciple is maintained only as other camouflaged perils are recognized and avoided.

The first is pride. The Word of God says, "Pride goeth before destruction" (Proverbs 16:18). We need to ask God to search our hearts and root out this subtle peril that has time and again ruined Christian men. I have seen young men, dedicated, zealous, filled with the Spirit, and seemingly being used by God, become totally ineffective because of pride. They have seen answers to prayer and are sure they are getting through to God. Or they have been greatly used by God in the salvation of souls. Or they have been told that they are exceptionally gifted in some way. Then spiritual conceit invades and takes over.

One mark of spiritual and emotional stability is to remain unaffected by commendation. Such a person can take the praise and honor of men realistically. He knows where the true honor is due.

The unstable person receives praise and clutches it protectively. If he is told he is weak in a particular area, he will nurse the memory of someone telling him this was his strong point! A balanced Christian knows how to accept the praise of men with diffidence and to welcome their criticism with concern. When you begin to accomplish something for God, watch for pride to follow and repent of it before the cross.

There is a kind of pride that elevates us while debasing others. We must be careful of criticizing Christians for not having attained something spiritual which we believe we have gained. But we have not gained it if we indeed do possess it; we have received it from God.

It helps me sometimes to think what I will be like forty years from now: will I preach with as much zeal, as much urgency, as much exercise of spirit as now? I can't know, and I must be careful what I say about others.

Someone has pointed out to me that the defects which we sometimes see and judge in others may be battle-scars suffered in faithful service to Christ. Perhaps the Christian has seen more and harder battles than we. He may have won many battles, but not without scars and wounds in the process.

We might consider older men of God old-fashioned and short on zeal. Younger Christians must show mercy to the older generation, and I ask them in return to have mercy in their dealings with us. God wants both the older and younger generations to realize neither would be anything without Christ and his grace.

The kindred peril to pride is a critical spirit. It seems easy to see distinctly everything that is wrong with other people. But psychologists tell us that the things we most readily criticize in others are sometimes things which are wrong in our own lives. This is called projection, and some Christians unwittingly specialize in it.

When I tested myself on this, the results scared me. If, day in and day out, I was seeing something wrong in other people, was it really a reflection of some weakness in my own personality or habits? I saw others' inconsistencies so readily. One man tended to be superficial; another seemed to say things that he did not mean; a third was weak on economizing time. But could it be true that these weaknesses supposedly contrasted with my strengths, but the comparison was neither fair nor kind.

Paul instructed Christians in Philippians 4 to think positively:

"Finally, brethren, whatsoever things are true, whatsoever things are honest, whatsoever things are just, whatsoever things are pure, whatsoever things are lovely, whatsoever things are of good report, if there be any virtue and if there be any praise, think on these things."

I believe this represents part of the revolution in men's lives that Christ came to bring. It is a revolution that replaces complaint with wholesome and affirmative thinking, a revolution that passes over people's mistakes and follies to bring God's light and love on the scene.

One time I was running to catch a train in Stockholm and hot criticism welled up within me against the brother who had mixed up the schedule and got me to the station ten minutes after the train was due to leave. "Why cannot people who have lived in Stockholm all their lives read their timetables?" I thought to myself. I wanted to get to Gothenberg the next morning in order to investigate a ship that might serve our goal of world evangelism.

I left the station, battling with myself, until the Lord brought Romans 8:28 to my mind. Some might say that this verse is a "crutch" for the crippled, but I was feeling crippled as I sought victory over the feelings in my heart. I leaned on the promise: "All things work together for good to them that love God, to those who are the called according to his purpose." And in faith I was able to praise God that I did not catch the train.

That night the train I had missed crashed. I offer no explanation for the crash, but I learned to be more careful about concluding that disappointing events are mistakes. We make mistakes, but our God does not. And with infinite patience and foresight, he specializes in overruling ours.

The Bible tells us God has entrusted the treasures of the Holy Spirit to the clay pots of our bodies as containers. In our work for the Lord we often mess up his purpose. There are times when I could weep for marring the wonder of his truth with my corroded personality, my beat-up pot. But God's sovereign power overrules and makes the crudest, weakest, lowliest, most out-of-place testimony for him count for eternity.

If we have a greater vision of our sovereign God, our negativeness and criticism would diminish or vanish. When we fully realize that our human leaders are learners like the rest of us, we can concentrate on God and be delivered from a critical spirit.

Another peril to the victorious Christian is becoming accustomed to spiritual things. As we see the power of God at work, answering prayer and accomplishing the impossible in people's lives, we may find ourselves being callous about the miraculous.

A team working in Operation Mobilization met for prayer in Zaventem, Belgium, and quite a few stayed to pray until 3 A.M. The financial needs of the work were acute and God stirred us to a great exercise of faith. When we went to bed, we had a thrilling consciousness that God was going to work. The next morning I had to phone our central office in England for some other business. On the phone someone asked me if I had heard about the large gift which had come from another country. The telegram announcing the gift had come into our office that very day. The amount was some $6,000. The money did not come from someone who was stirred up in the prayer meeting, but from someone thousands of miles away, who had sent it sometime earlier. We have seen things like this happen for over a decade, and we simply praise God for his answers to prayer. But there is a grave danger of becoming familiar with the miraculous, casual about God moving in wonderful ways.

The Bible says that there is rejoicing in the presence of the angels over one soul that repents, but sometimes we do not rejoice unless it is a dozen. I remember at Bible College when I went out and was able to help someone find Christ. I really got excited and would barge into a fellow student's room bubbling with joy. "Come on, drop your work. Let's have a prayer meeting, brother. Let's give up some time to praise the Lord." A week later, another brother would come to see me. He was not as loudmouthed as I: "Praise the Lord, George; a fellow down the street accepted Christ tonight." What was my reaction? "Oh, praise God; that's good. Amen." And back I went to my studies. May God forgive us for letting ourselves become over-familiar with holy things, or rejoice over our victory and not over that of the other fellow.

Such familiarity can be heartbreaking in gatherings of God's people. Sometimes we meet around the Lord's Table to remember his death and there is less praise among us than if we shared a meal of ham and eggs after a long night. The Israelites in the wilderness took God's miracles for granted: they became accustomed to manna, and craved meat. God gave them the meat they desired, and leanness filled their souls. It can happen to us, too.

Another peril of the Christian life is asceticism. If we seek hardship because it builds our reputation, we are not suffering for Christ's sake. An example of this was a young man on a witnessing tour who was invited to stay overnight at a Christian home where the hostess went to a lot of trouble to prepare a comfortable bed. The young man stiffened proudly and announced that he no longer slept in beds. He had forgotten — or had never learned — that Paul knew how both to be abased and to abound. This balance is difficult, but it is possible as we make love our way and Christ our goal.

Asceticism is not nearly such a problem as its opposite — laziness and the love of ease. This is one of the most deadly perils for a Christian in the position of independent responsibility. Discipline is good for us, and laziness is a great sin. One reason the Church lacks foot soldiers is that it lacks people who want to work hard. Nehemiah's men finished their task because they had a "mind to work." When the pressures of duties relax, laziness becomes a tremendous danger to many Christians.

Then there is the serious peril of disqualification. When God begins to use you significantly, the devil closes in to discover some flaw that he can exploit and scandalize. Evangelist Alan Redpath has pointed out that King David's sin with Bathsheba was preceded by his sinful withdrawal from battle. While his troops were fighting the enemy, he was at leisure, and his relaxation physically and spiritually opened him to the whirlwind of temptation that swept him into sinful lust and God's judgment.

This illustrates the peril of being away from the place God has called us to, of breaking communion with the Lord Jesus Christ, of self-indulgence, and of arrogant criticism. These give Satan his chance to invade our spirit and inflame sin that will dishonor God and ruin our testimony. Though the sin can be forgiven, the consequences may hinder the gospel for years.

Perils still beset the Christian living in the Promised Land, and we must be aware of them. We must remember the warning in 1 Corinthians 10:12: "Let him that thinketh he standeth take heed lest he fall." God's provision for us amid the dangers is constant: "There hath no temptation taken you but such as is common to man; but God is faithful . . . he will make a way of escape" (10:13). Choose it, and God's grace will bring victory.

6

LOVE THAT CONQUERS

In John 13:34, 35 we read these words of Jesus: "A new commandment I give unto you, That you love one another; as I have loved you, that you also love one another. By this shall all men know that you are my disciples, if you have love one to another." This is the touchstone of Christianity and the dynamic of the revolution that was begun by Jesus Christ himself.

Some Christians seem to have misread this verse. They apparently see: "By this shall all men know that you are my disciples, that you have no possessions." Or ". . . that you read and carry your Bibles." Or perhaps ". . . that you have sound doctrine." Or maybe that ". . . you traverse land and sea to win converts to Christ."

But Jesus said none of those things. He said that there is one major thing that will convince the world we are his disciples, and that is the love we have for one another. We are not the disciples of a theory or doctrine or institution, but disciples of the loving Jesus! His love led Jesus to give his life for us, and that kind of love is commanded between Jesus' followers.

People sometimes ask me, "How do you conceive of the love of God?" My answer is found in 1 John 3:16 — "In this we perceive the love of God, in that he laid down his life for us." As a consequence, says John, "So we ought to lay down our lives for the brethren." This is the supreme love, Jesus told us, for "greater love has no man than this, that a man lay down his life for his friends" (John 15:13).

Love is the essence of discipleship: it is the wall that surrounds a disciple, the roof that protects him, and the ground which supports him. The Bible says emphatically that though I speak with tongues of men and of angels, have all wisdom, make tremendous sacrifices, give my body to be burned, and relinquish all I own, I am worth nothing if I have not done them in love.

Most of us have to admit that we know very

little about actually loving people. We know that we have often loved because of the benefits that come to us. Divine love is impartial; it loves the repulsive and the attractive, the beggar and the merchant prince.

Is this love really possible? And does it work? When I give myself for the sake of another, when I "fall into the ground and die" in order to bear fruit, when I deny myself and take up the cross and follow Jesus — does it make a revolutionary difference? Or would it turn me into a blind fanatic rushing from one good deed to another and getting trampled by the strong?

This love is possible, and it is very practical. It does not come naturally, nor does it come instantly in a rededication service or some particular experience. Real love comes from God, who is love, and it is developed in the hard school of life over many years. There may be a crisis of appropriating God's love, but a process of expressing love follows or it all becomes an abscess.

The Bible speaks clearly on how to acquire and develop God's love. The first thing it tells me is that love is a fruit of the Spirit (Galatians 5:22). As every Christian has the Spirit, every Christian may have this love. Ephesians 5:18 gives one of the few commands about the Holy Spirit in the New Testament: "Be not drunk with wine, wherein is excess; but be filled with the Spirit." The filling produces an overflow that touches other people.

What are evidences of the filling of the Spirit? ". . . Speaking to [among] yourselves in psalms and hymns and spiritual songs." This is joy and encouragement shared with other Christians. And it also communicates with God: ". . . singing and making melody in your hearts to the Lord; giving thanks always for all things." These signs accompany the love given by the Holy Spirit.

The Scriptures also teach that prayer will develop this love. Paul is our example: "I bow my knees unto the Father of our Lord Jesus Christ . . . that he would grant you . . . to be strengthened by his Spirit . . . and to know the love of Christ, which passeth knowledge" (Ephesians 3:14, 16, 19).

As the Lord blesses the person prayed for, he will also work in your heart. We are sometimes partly responsible for others' weaknesses, and weaknesses in a brother's life may reflect weaknesses in our own. If I have been spiritually discerning of something wrong, through prayer I can help to change it. Let us pray earnestly for the people we do not like or do not understand, and God will make changes in the situation. We have many examples of this in Scripture, and we are exhorted to pray for all men, even our enemies, said the Lord Jesus.

Another helpful step is to pray with the person concerned. If you are having trouble with someone in your church or group, try to pray with him about various needs and joys. This effort to share and understand will be rewarded by fellowship and a growing love.

The love of God believes the best about people, and discounts adverse reports and rumors. Love sympathizes and assists. Perhaps there are intense problems handicapping the person. Poor health may be dragging him down. Background environment or heredity may still control the individual. Prayer together can open the channel of love and wisdom from God to both.

Belief in the sovereignty of God enables us to rest in the confidence that he is in charge of all that is going on in the earth. Sometimes the devil seems menacingly near, but he is weak in comparison with the God who is in charge of our lives. Though Satan makes headway, he cannot overcome the Christian who is trusting God. He can say, "The Lord is in this," and look for the Lord's way out. Philippians 1:6 assures us that God has begun his work in us, and he will complete it.

Another step that develops love is personal interest in the welfare of others. This is shown by both words and deeds. Sincere attention builds a bond that involves us in others' lives. If someone's personality rubs against yours, ask questions about your common concerns and look for things to compliment. You'll find love sprouting from the interest, and you may receive love in return.

Some of us find it easy to make fun of people: the shape of their ears, the style of clothes, or the odd mannerisms. Jokes about others are good fun unless they wound the victim. Amy Carmichael said:

"If I enjoy a joke at the expense of another, if I can in any way slight another in conversation or even in thought, then I know nothing of Calvary love. If I belittle those whom I am called to serve, talk of their weak points in contrast to what I think are my strong points; if I adopt a superior attitude, forgetting 'Who made thee to differ? What hast thou that thou didst not receive?' then I know nothing of Calvary love."

Another stimulus to love is to give something to another. There is a story of a husband and wife whose marriage was on the rocks. The husband never remembered anniversaries or birthdays, and he was always complaining. She became more and more discouraged. One day he inexplicably decided to bring her some flowers. It was so unusual that when he came to the door and held out the flowers she wept hysterically. "What a miserable day!" she moaned. "I've been having trouble with the children all day, the clothes washer broke, I burned the supper, and now you've come home drunk!" Don't wait so long to rebuild a relationship that your gift can't be believed! Give something of practical help or a memento that shows you care.

How blind we sometimes are to the plain words of Scripture! Jesus commanded the help of his people to one another by saying: "Inasmuch as ye have done it unto one of the least of these my brethren, ye have done it unto me" (Matthew 25:40). This is a revolutionary passage of Scripture, and if we let it penetrate our minds daily, it would change our lives. Our attitude toward the weak and the needy, God says, reveals our attitude to his Son. This should lead us to repentance. "He who loves not his brother whom he has seen, how can he love God whom he has not seen?" (1 John 4:20)

And have we forgotten what is called the Golden Rule? "Therefore all things whatsoever ye would that men should do unto you, do ye even so unto them: for this is the law and the prophets" (Matthew 7:12). This verse offers us a simple check on our speaking or acting: Would I enjoy this if it were directed at me? This would eliminate cruel gossip and destructive criticism, and would spare us from future judgment.

The Bible tells us we are to correct someone in the spirit of love when it is necessary. "Brethren, if a man be overtaken in a fault, ye which are spiritual" — which excludes quite a few Christians — "restore such an one in the spirit of meekness; considering thyself, lest thou also be tempted" (Galatians 6:1). Amy Carmichael wrote: "If we can go to someone to correct them without a pang in our hearts, then we know nothing of Calvary love." The love depicted in 1 Corinthians 13 allows no rejoicing hearts over the failure of another person. Love never speaks with the attitude: "I told you so; you should have listened to me!" It sorrows with those who mourn, and lifts up those who fall.

In his love, God can transform sorrows and failure so we can help and comfort others. God, says Paul, "comforteth us in all our tribulation, that we may be able to comfort them which are in any trouble, by the comfort wherewith we ourselves are comforted of God" (2 Corinthians 1:4). How can a woman who has had four children, with no complications at birth and no problems as they have grown up, help a woman who has had three still births and now has a handicapped child? She has not been prepared for this opportunity. But a woman who has lost a child herself or has suffered deeply in some other way can communicate the love of God that she has experienced. She may speak directly, but with compassion, to the sufferer.

To rebuke and exhort another Christian is one of the hardest things to do properly. It is easier to overlook the fault, but love must correct at times. Amy Carmichael comments: "If I'm

73

afraid to speak the truth lest I lose affection or lest the one concerned should say, 'You do not understand,' or because I fear to lose my reputation for kindness; if I put my own name before the other's highest good, then I know nothing of Calvary love."

Love acts. When I see a little child running toward a busy street, I do not just stand there and suggest: "Wouldn't it be better to stay on the pavement?" I move into action. I grab the child back from the street in order that its life may be saved. The Bible says that we are to snatch men from the fire of hell. To think such action too drastic is a misconception of love.

The love of Jesus was not of the Hollywood variety. His love led him to serve. I believe it was also love that sent Jesus into the Temple to clean up the mercenary mess there and to chase out the greedy merchants with violence. It was love for righteousness; it was love for those who were being cheated. His love led to action all through his life.

Love grows — when it is exercised. Supplying all-conquering love is God's part; expressing love is our part. As we walk with God, he will make us confident "of this very thing, that he which hath begun a good work in you will perform it until the day of Jesus Christ" (Philippians 1:6). And God will work in the lives of others by love, for his perfect love never fails.

7

WHEN I AM WEAK . . .

Many young people begin Christian service believing that they are dedicated and keen Christians. They have been encouraged to think so by their complimentary friends or church officers. And perhaps they did rise above the average Christian in their surroundings. But service on the firing line makes them more and more conscious of Jesus' words: "Without me you can do nothing" (John 15:5).

All Christian workers come eventually — if they are honest — to the place where they can no longer casually affirm their dedication to the

Lord. They realize only too well that they are not Hudson Taylor or George Mueller or C. T. Studd. The result may be extreme depression: since great exploits constantly elude them, they may conclude that there is no hope for them.

There is an antidote for this. Robert Murray M'Cheyne once said that for every look he took at himself, he took ten looks at the Lord Jesus. He had abandoned hope in himself, but his hope in Christ was boundless! For M'Cheyne and for us, total failure may be necessary to bring us to the realization our only hope is in Jesus! And it is not Jesus plus money, or Jesus plus an efficient organization, or the proper equipment, but only Jesus!

Thanks to the Apostle Paul, we have an example who has proved this way to victory. "And he said to me, My grace is sufficient for thee; for my strength is made perfect in weakness. Most gladly therefore will I rather glory in my infirmities, that the power of Christ may rest upon me" (2 Corinthians 12:9).

When you are in a tight situation, when the demons of discord, criticism, misunderstanding, and confusion maul you in a pressure cooker, remember those words: "My grace is sufficient for thee." Without this knowledge and confidence, you cannot survive the warfare that awaits the disciple of Christ.

Can the cost of Christian warfare be less than

that of nations in conflict? If it is, it is not warfare. Alexander Duff, the Scottish saint of God, knew the cost. Weeping as he faced a crowd, he asked if Scotland had any more sons to give. "When Queen Victoria calls for volunteers for India, hundreds respond," he reminded them. "But when King Jesus calls, no one goes." The silence was deafening. "If there is no one who will go," he continued, "then I will return. I will return and lay my bones by the Ganges, that India may know that Scotland has at least one who cares."

Whether we remain at home or go abroad, Christ's claim upon our lives is a call to battle. The enemy is powerful; he is dragging and tricking souls into hell; he is devastating the hopes and plans of men on earth. Yet Jesus can defeat him through any Christian who puts on the spiritual armor (Ephesians 6:11-18). Our hope, then, is in the all-sufficient Lord Jesus, not in ourselves. Whatever the circumstances: "My grace is sufficient for thee," promised God.

Someone has said that "grace is God's riches at Christ's expense." This definition underlines the great gift imparted to us by Christ. It is the riches of the infinite God, inherited through the death and resurrection of his Son. It is all too easy to become indifferent to what Jesus did on the cross. It is all too possible to gather thoughtlessly around the Lord's Table. When this happens, we void the riches of the grace of God!

There is another way of voiding God's grace: we do this by underrating it. If we get to the point of desperation and say, "O God, what's the use? I can't go any further — and you can't help me, either," we deny the grace of God. And just at that moment, we could discover his grace, his sufficiency, his life, and his power are available to take us through. This is tragic and sinful.

The demands and standards of Christ are admittedly extreme — in fact, impossible. But Jesus does not ask us to live the Christian life; he asks us to let him live it in us. There was no grace for the self-righteous man who prayed, "Thank you, Lord, that I'm not like the rest." But there was grace for the man who wept, "I'm a sinner; Lord, have mercy on me!" The complete sufficiency of the Lord Jesus Christ makes up for our deficiency. We cannot earn his grace; we can get it only by coming empty to the cross.

Paul speaks an amazing truth in Colossians 2: 9-10: "For in him (Christ) dwelleth all the fullness of the Godhead bodily. And you are complete in him." Complete! Do we realize this when we strive to build a reputation? Do we realize it when someone deprives us of recognition? Do we realize it when we feel uncomfortable in a group? Perhaps we feel worse when we suffer persecution or ill health for serving God. Or we may languish in jail for righteousness' sake.

Our plans fail; our witness is rejected. How do we feel then?

You *are complete in Christ!* Our completeness is not in Christ plus friends, Christ plus service, Christ plus position, Christ plus converts. We are complete only in Jesus! In him is all the fullness, so Jesus is all that we need. Everything else may fail us; Jesus will never leave nor forsake us.

Whatever arises that might discourage us, we can echo with the conviction of Paul: Jesus is sufficient for that, too. The question is not in his sufficiency, but only in our trusting him. We cannot go on, we just will not make it! We may want to quit: the Lord is asking too much of us! Each time, *he is sufficient.* He says to us, "You are complete in me." We have been made acceptable to God in Christ the Beloved One.

We all seek acceptance; all of us want to be needed, liked, cared for. If we expect we are going to meet the ideal husband or wife to meet those needs, we are going to be disappointed. Not even a husband or wife can fulfil our heart's deepest longings, because we were made for God. Only he can reach down and fill that deep void; only he can satisfy.

In Jesus Christ, we have been accepted by God *now.* We have been accepted, not by some social group, but by the infinite *God.* We have been accepted, not in our spotted virtue, but in the perfect Lord Jesus Christ. With this confidence motivating us, nothing in the heights or depths, in life or death, nor in the whole universe can stop us, for nothing can withstand him. His grace, abundant and overflowing, is ours — if we will receive it.

STEPS TO REVOLUTION!

Having read these pages, you might be asking yourself: "What do I do next?" To read about the all-sufficiency of Jesus Christ is one thing; to obtain and experience it in your own life is another.

More than anything, this book is a plea and a guide for reality in the Christian life. The standard of vital Christianity described in these pages will not be reached easily. It will not occur through a short prayer of commitment or by any kind of crisis experience. God may use a crisis to jolt a Christian into action, but *a crisis plus a process* is necessary to keep him moving as a revolutionary disciple of Jesus Christ.

If this book is to be significant to you, you must "*declare a personal revolution.*" This will take all your dedication and the application of every means of grace offered in the Word of God. There cannot be a revolution for those who merely "play the game" or go through the motions. Nor is revolution possible for the Christian who is not willing to deny self, take up his cross daily, and follow Jesus.

We are not ready for revolution if we have not yet seen the spiritual schizophrenia within and around us. God must convince us that "the heart is deceitful above all things, and desperately wicked." Spiritual fog seeps into our hearts from the world, and only God can dispel it in response to earnest prayer.

To be ready for revolution, we must accept the blame for not living a dynamic Christian life. Christ lives within the Christian, and *he* is the revolutionary. We must be willing to die to self-interests and self-determination and let Christ live his life through us.

Many Christians are entering the ministry and the mission fields and other places of Christian service without being spiritually prepared. We must realize that we are in dangerous territory if our service for God is taking us beyond our experience of God. Satan waits there to attack us — and we are very vulnerable. The revolutionary spiritual life issues from a deep relationship and experience with God, who makes the disciple a faithful soldier of Christ.

I am absolutely convinced that Christians who take the following steps to revolution will find that they "work." They work because Christianity works. These steps are basic biblical principles which Jesus Christ and the apostles repeatedly emphasized to those who wanted to be disciples of Jesus.

1. *A revolution in our prayer life.* One of the most depressing signs in the Church today is the lack of prayer, both in private and in groups. It is almost incredible to see how little the average evangelical church relies on prayer for doing God's work. When there is a prayer meeting, a small minority of the people are involved. Nights of prayer, home prayer meetings, days of prayer and fasting — so much a part of the early Church — seem nothing more than Christian relics today. Because people are busy, they think they are too busy to pray. The Church has sought innumerable substitutes for prayer to accomplish work that can be done *only* through prayer.

If we are serious about being spiritual revolutionaries, we must determine to learn how to pray! There are many excellent books on the subject, but there is no substitute for getting on our knees and starting to pray. Samuel Chadwick said, "The one concern of the devil is to keep the saints from prayer. He fears nothing from prayerless studies, prayerless work, prayerless religion. He laughs at our toil, mocks at our wisdom, but trembles when we pray."

The mountain peak of our prayer life will be worship. Specific times should be given each day to climbing the summit of spiritual reality through worship, praise, and thanksgiving. King David declared, "I will praise the name of God with a song, and will magnify him with thanksgiving. This also shall please the Lord better than an ox or bullock that hath horns and hoofs" (Psalm 69:30, 31).

Reality in worship will create a spiritual revolution in the inner man, the likes of which few people seem to have experienced in the twentieth century. It will not be attained in a year or two, nor perhaps in ten or twenty years. However, since this is the highest calling of the Christian, it is worth any number of years to learn reality in daily worship. There is no more important aspect of spiritual revolution than this.

There is a sense in which we can "pray without ceasing" and offer prayer and praise to God at any time of the day. Yet there is also a need for separating ourselves from other humans and being alone with God. The entire Church and the cause of Christ around the world is suffering for lack of this kind of prayer. If the only response made to this book were a determination to take a definite time each day for prayer, praise, and feasting on God's Word, the book would be eminently successful. For through prayer, we can come to see the other principles of spiritual revolution which will lead us from victory to victory as God's Word is mixed with our faith.

2. *A revolution in our Bible study.* At any cost, spiritual revolutionaries must become "men of the Book." D. L. Moody declared, "Either sin will keep you from this Book, or this Book will keep you from sin." Most Christians place a low value on memorizing and meditating on the Word of God. In contrast, Muslims by the thousands leave their universities with the whole Koran memorized. Actors and actresses memorize thousands of lines to earn fame and wealth. Despite the spiritual rewards promised for students of God's Word, few Christians seek them. The result is churches peopled by spiritual dwarfs, some having been "growing" ten or twenty years in the faith.

In some cases spiritual dwarfs become leaders of the congregation, and the contrast with New Testament churches is shocking. If anyone points this out, he is regarded as a fanatic, an extremist, or a meddler.

On the other hand, I have found increasing numbers of believers around the world who are tired of eating spiritual breadcrumbs and want to get into God's Word in a new and revolutionary way. The important thing, however, is not so much our "getting into the Word of God" as "the Word of God getting into us"! This means we must engage in more than Bible reading; we must meditate intensively on the Word of God, as the Psalmist instructs in 119:9, 11.

Our Bible study must be as honest and unprejudiced as possible. We cannot come to the Word of God with our favorite viewpoint and expect the Bible to shed new light. We must come to the Scriptures in humility and openness, and attempt to obey in our daily living each truth we find there.

An evangelist has warned: "We have taken the Word of God, the Sword of the Spirit, and used it to carve one another up instead of going forth in a great offensive in the name of Christ." How much easier it is to go to war over pet doctrines and favorite verses rather than continuing to receive the whole counsel of God, and advancing against the enemy.

We must not only determine to obey those verses we enjoy, or that strike us as being important, but we must be ready to obey verses that sometimes strike us in the opposite way.

We are sometimes eager to accept those verses that speak about blessing and to neglect verses that speak about suffering. We welcome the first part of 1 John 3:16, "Hereby perceive we the love of God, because he laid down his life for us" — and the rest trails through and out of our consciousness: ". . . and we ought to lay down our lives for the brethren." The next admonition also gets scant attention: "But whoso hath this world's good, and seeth his brother have need, and shutteth up his bowels of compassion from him, how dwelleth the love of God in him?"

This is also God's Word! What excuse do we have for our failure to "love not merely in word but in deed and in truth"? Obedience here is revolution!

3. *A revolution of discipline.* For many, discipline is an unpleasant word. Yet church history shows no undisciplined man or woman who amounted to much for Christ. The basic support of discipline is motivation, and the best motivation is the constraining love of Christ.

Christ said, "If ye love me, keep my commandments." He also said, "If ye continue in my words, then are ye my disciples indeed." This is critical, as we can realize from Paul's concern in 1 Corinthians 9:26, 27: "I therefore so run, not as uncertainly; so fight I, not as one that beateth the air: but I keep under my body, and bring it into subjection: lest that by any means, when I have preached to others, I myself should be a castaway." Paul was disciplined but he recognized the danger of slipping and falling into sin.

True discipline is possible only because of the promises of God. We find ourselves unable to keep a particular commandment or engage in a form of self-discipline, but we can be sustained by such a promise as: "I can do all things through Christ which strengtheneth me" (Philippians 4:13). For every battle and difficulty in life, there is an assurance of God's grace and sufficiency we can claim.

We are hearing more and more in Christian circles about a victorious life being attained through a particular sanctification theory or crisis experience which launches an effortless joyride with God. But for every Bible verse that speaks of rest, abiding, trusting, and allowing God to work through you there is another word nearby that speaks of battle, testing, obedience, and the need to present our bodies as a living sacrifice to do God's will. These are complementary and essential for the balanced life.

We do not pit Joshua against Caleb because they used different terminology and concepts to challenge the people to enter the Promised Land. The spiritual revolutionary learns the balance between God's action and his own. He depends on God's strength and wisdom to work out the salvation life within him.

For example, if you lie in bed tomorrow morning and pray that the Lord will lift you out of bed, you are likely to have a very late breakfast! The recital of "Not I, but Christ" will bring about few changes unless you *move*. But when you move, the recognition of "Not I, but Christ" will produce eternal results by God's Spirit.

One of the important disciplines is repentance. When we sin or fail, we can recover and go on if we immediately find forgiveness at the cross. Many a Christian has languished in depression and defeat because he hadn't learned the discipline of repentance. Not even Jesus Christ "felt" like going to the cross, but he went because he loved us and was obedient to the will of God. We may not "feel" like going to the cross, but we will because of our love for Christ. There we receive total forgiveness and joyous renewal that will enable us to live in discipline.

4. *A revolution of love.* Jesus Christ said that people would know Christians were his disciples because of their *love* for one another. The greatest indictment of evangelical Christianity is that Christians have failed to have this kind of love. Yet when I have seen this love in a few Christians, it has impressed me as the expression of genuine Christianity.

It is amazing to see how the Lord Jesus Christ can change an unloving, lost soul. In country after country I have seen the power of this revolution of love. If more of us would enter in and fan the flames of this love, I believe we would see spiritual revolution around the world in our generation. This does not necessarily mean the conversion of masses of people, but rather individuals everywhere transformed by the revolutionary principles of the New Testament and living them before others.

Unless we "declare a revolution" in the areas of life already mentioned, however, we will not see a revolution of love. For it is only as we get to know God at a deep level and trust Christ to work through us that we can receive and demonstrate revolutionary love. Until we do experience this love, the spiritual revolution will not reach very far.

Nothing obstructs revolutionary Christianity like the opposite of love: resentment, envy, anger, fear, jealousy, and hatred. The mutual toleration evidenced in handshakes after the typical Sunday morning church service also falls far short of the revolutionary love that unites brethren in dynamic fellowship. Yet a greater display of interest in one another is not the real answer; revolutionary love is the outcome of obedience to and communion with Christ.

The greatest possible impact on the world would be made if Christians of many races, backgrounds, churches, and temperaments were working together in love and harmony with Jesus as King and Lord. The Bible says, "Love casteth out fear," and we could move forward on that promise, finding that divine love would cast fear out of our hearts — the fear of people we do not understand, who are from a different race, or who worship differently. We must break out of our cliques and work with all of God's people. We must unite under the banner of Christ's love and the cardinal doctrines and principles of New Testament Christianity. The pride that scorns Christians outside "our group" will have to die at the cross before we can join in revolution. If any of us has received more light, exercised more gifts, or been granted more recognition, it should be demonstrated by more humility and more love.

This is the essential principle of Christian living and spiritual revolution; without it, there is no power.

5. *A revolution of honesty*. Spiritual honesty is one of our greatest needs. We evangelicals have grown accustomed to our religious masks, pretending to be one thing while living quite another. It has continued so long that we hardly know now where reality is. Can you imagine what a revolution of honesty would do in our churches? If we were honest, many of us would have to change the words of "Onward Christian Soldiers" in somewhat the following manner:

> Backward Christian soldiers, fleeing from the fight,
> With the cross of Jesus nearly out of sight:
> Christ our rightful Master stands against the foe,
> But forward into battle we are loathe to go.

Like a mighty tortoise moves the Church
of God;
Brothers, we are treading where we've often
trod,
We are much divided, many bodies we,
Having different doctrines, not much charity.

Crowns and thrones may perish, kingdoms
rise and wane,
But the Church of Jesus hidden does remain;
Gates of hell should never 'gainst that Church
prevail,
We have Christ's own promise, but think that
it will fail.

Sit here, then, ye people, join our useless
throngs;
Blend with ours your voices in a feeble song.
Blessings, ease and comfort, ask from Christ
the King,
With our modern thinking, we won't do a
thing.

These words might seem harsh, but you will
find stronger words in the New Testament. "I
know thy works, that thou art neither cold nor
hot: I would thou wert cold or hot. So, then, because thou art lukewarm, and neither cold nor
hot, I will spue thee out of my mouth. Because
thou sayest, I am rich, and increased with
goods, and have need of nothing; and knowest
not that thou art wretched and miserable, and
poor, and blind, and naked" (Revelation 3:15-
17).

We must declare war on that kind of self-deception described in these verses. To do this, we must determine to become spiritually honest. We must face ourselves as we are, and we must allow God to begin to bring revolutionary changes. Many of us are trying to live at a particular spiritual level when we know we are nowhere near it! This leads to all kinds of unreality, confusion, and sometimes even to nervous breakdown.

Sometimes the Christian most anxious to improve his spiritual life ends up with the greatest problems — because he tries to make the changes himself. The need is not for spiritual extremists, but for spiritual revolutionaries who know the reality of spiritual balance. The spiritual revolutionary knows that according to Ephesians 1: 6 he is fully accepted in the Beloved, and therefore he ceases striving to gain merit through his spiritual activity. He recognizes that he is a sinner, but in Christ he is a victor.

Christian leaders may fall into this trap quicker than the average Christian. When Christians make heroes of leaders, they may feel forced to act out their roles while despising their hypocrisy. It is a very unhealthy and precarious route to follow.

One of the reasons many Christian young people forsake the church and their parents is widespread spiritual pretense. A normal young person understands failures are inevitable, but continual inconsistency and spiritual dishonesty deeply confuse him. Some are so repelled by the double life that they "drop out." They would rather befriend an "honest" agnostic than live in the shadow of spiritual schizophrenia. A spiritual revolution may be necessary to recall these rebels to fellowship in the Church. I challenge the rebels to follow Christ and help spring this revolution.

6. *A revolution of witness.* When the revolution takes place in the areas described, it will spontaneously bring a revolution of witness. Half the world still remains in spiritual darkness as far as a knowledge of Jesus Christ is concerned.

When we have gone forth, we have often taken the nonrevolutionary form of Christianity. A. W. Tozer wrote: "The popular notion that the first obligation of the Church is to spread the gospel to the uttermost parts of the earth is false. Her first obligation is to be spiritually worthy to spread it. . . . To spread an effete, degenerate brand of Christianity to pagan lands is not to fulfill the commandments of the Lord."

Tozer was a twentieth-century prophet who spoke for God from the pulpit and through his books. If we put into practice the principles he set forth (allowing for human error), we would see a spiritual revolution. This in turn would lead to witnessing in every form which would gather many people into the Church of the Lord Jesus Christ. Down through history, men who had different theological perspectives have lived out the same kind of dynamic, revolutionary Christianity, and we should be able to lay down our doctrinal pop-guns and work together in world evangelism and spiritual revolution.

The Jehovah's Witnesses, with all their false doctrines, boast of being ninety percent mobile. That is, ninety percent of their membership is involved in definite outreach and witness. What can we say of our evangelical churches' mobility? In some churches it seems that only the pastor and perhaps a few others know how to win others to Christ. But the New Testament clearly teaches that each believer in Christ is a witness. The fact that people have come to Christ just through reading a piece of Christian literature should show us that no Christian need arrive in heaven without helping someone else get there.

There are many ways to witness and though some ways may be better than others, the teaching of Scripture is that we primarily witness through life and through word. Far more than a crusade, a special project, or outreach program, true witnessing is a spontaneous outflowing of the indwelling Christ.

Let's stop clutching our weaknesses, shyness, lack of training, fear, or any other excuse and start believing the God of the impossible who specializes in using weak vessels. There is not a single Christian who cannot become an effective, revolutionary witness for Jesus Christ if he really wants to.

In conclusion, I have two requests. The first is by far the more important. I request you to unite with me in repentance at the foot of the cross and *believe God* to bring into our lives and the lives of other Christians a spiritual revolution. Let us bow in daily repentance, recognizing our failures and believing God for great and dynamic changes in the days to come.

Second, I ask you to take a few minutes and write to me, care of the publisher, expressing what you feel after reading these pages. Perhaps this could be your first act of discipline after reading this book. I have a tremendous desire to pray for anyone who truly wants a spiritual revolution in his own heart and life. Those of us who want spiritual revolution in the twentieth century must unite and work together toward this goal. God is on our side — and if he is for us, who can be against us!